Comming soc

More designs projects

Table of Contents

INTRODUCTION 5

TERMINOLOGY.. 6

TECHNIQUES 8

MATERIALS 10

BASIC STROKES 12

LETTERS 18

CONNECTIONS & WORDS 70

EMBELLISHMENTS & ILLUSTRATIONS 91

DESIGN COMPOSITION 104

PROJECTS 108

INTRODUCTION

Calligraphy is a traditional art form that goes back thousands of years. Since it has been developed and modified by a vast range of social and technological changes, providing a rich and varied resource for the modern calligraphy.

If you've ever wanted to learn how to do modern calligraphy, but you weren't sure how to begin, this is the book that guides you towards your hobby. Here you will learn the essential skills and techniques, discover the different ways you can execute your ideas and find many suggestions for practicing the skills you learned in a way that is fun and relaxing. You will find for you a source of inspiration for allowing your own beautiful writing to flow by applying a variety of lettering styles in sake of creating beautiful artwork.

This book is free from all kinds of complications and long explanations that might make you give up entering the art of calligraphy. Instead, it will encourage you to find your own creative style of making calligraphy and hand lettering.

Inside, you'll find a set of styles and ideas you can use as reference in creating your own work. We've also featured some designs with different lettering styles that will inspire you even more.

Happy lettering!

TERMINOLOGY

Before we get started learning calligraphy and hand lettering styles, let's get familiar with some commonly used terms (basic terms) that help to introduce with an easy and comprehensive way the art of calligraphy and hand lettering.

1 BASELINE

The line where the letters sit.

A B a b

2 MIDLINE

The line in between the baseline and the cap line.

a c e n

3 ASCENDER

The part of the letter that goes above the midline, such as for letters b, k, and t.

b d k

4 DESCENDER

The part of the letter that falls below the baseline, such as for letters g, q, and y.

g p q

5 FLOURISH

The added strokes and swashes used to decorate or enhance letters.

6 SERIF

Small decorative strokes extending from the main body of a letterform.

7 SANS-SERIF

A letter without any extending features.

8 UPSTROKE

The part of the letter that you move your pen up to make (thin line).

Upwards = less pressure

9 DOWNTROKE

The part of the letter that you push your pen down to make (thick line).

Downwards = more pressure

10 CROSS STROKE

Horizontal strokes on letters such as t, and uppercase A, H, and F.

11 OVERTURN STROKE

To create the Overturn stroke start with a thin upstroke that transitions into a thick downstroke. This stroke can be found in the letters m and n.

12 UNDERTURN STROKE

To create this stroke start with a thick downstroke that transitions into a thin upstroke. This stroke can be found in the letters a, i, and u.

13 X-HEIGHT
The height of a lowercase letter.

14 SCRIPT
Letters joined together in a continuous, fluid motion (i.e. cursive).

15 LETTERFORM:
The shape of a letter.

TECHNIQUES

In this chapter, we introduce the inherent concepts and the associated terminology that form the foundation of hand lettering to clarify all the questions that comes into mind when entering this art . You'll discover the variety of letter styles presented in this book, and the very first steps you need to know for proper letter formation.

HAND LETTERING

Hand lettering, as the name suggests, is the art of drawing letters by hand. It's called "art" because we draw each letter as if it was a piece of art. Hand lettering has fewer rules than calligraphy for how artists use particular scripts or styles, it considers stylization and overall composition more important, also tools and styles can be mixed and matched to create unique, expressive text that can be developed into a variety of artworks.

Hand lettering encompasses a variety of styles and techniques, many of which we're going to look at together in the coming sections.
The most common hand lettering styles are: Serif, Sans-serif, and monoline.

 ## SERIF

The small decorative lines at the foot or head of the letters are called serifs. There are many different shapes of Serifs.

 ## MONOLINE

Monoline is a style in which the line remains the same weight from beginning to end (The line weight stays consistent).

 ## SANS-SERIF

Sans ("Sans" means "without") serif is kind of the opposite of serif and refers to letters that do not have a serif at the foot or the head.

 ## FAUX CALLIGRAPHY

Faux calligraphy refers to creating a calligraphy-like style with a normal pen or pencil.

CALLIGRAPHY

The word calligraphy originated from the Greek words for "beauty" and "to write" which means: "beautiful writing". By contrast to hand lettering, calligraphy is the art of writing stylized letters, and is solely based on penmanship. It relies on disciplined practice and muscle memory, and requires simple, smooth lines created through the repetitive strokes used to write each letter.

Calligraphy

 ## MODERN

Modern calligraphy is any style that does not follow the fundamental rules of traditional calligraphy scripts such as copperplate, spencerian, italic, etc. modern calligraphy relies on certain principles of traditional calligraphy. However, it allows for experimentation and provides you with more creative freedom by mixing and matching letters and flourish styles.

BRUSH LETTERING

Brush lettering is calligraphy created using a brush pen or paint brush by applying varying degrees of pressure to achieve the thin and thick strokes of letters (Brush lettering is a form of modern calligraphy, except that, rather than using a flexible nib, brush pens use a flexible brush or marker tips).

Brush lettering

 ## TRADITIONAL

Traditional calligraphy is done with specific tools (like a pointed pen), and with precise measures of heights and angles. It's very structured, and flows standard rules with regard to letter height, spacing, placement...traditional calligraphy involves the execution of letters in a designated order and format.

In this book, we will cover some of these styles and put them to use by creating super beautiful, real designs.

MATERIALS

There are a lot of different varieties of tools you can use for hand lettering, so make sure to pick the best option that match your needs. Here are some of the basic tools and supplies you'll need with short description.

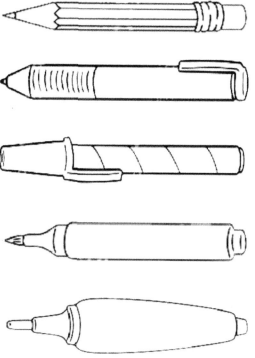

1. **Pencils:** First tool for sketching. Calligraphy can be created with pencils, but not all pencils are up to the challenge. Pencils which they have a soft graphite core are the best.

2. **Pens:** Pens are good for monoline style and faux calligraphy. There are so many great pens such as: Micron pens, gel pens...

3. **Brush pens:** Brush pens are great to begin your lettering journey. There are both small and large brush pens, and the tip range from stiff to flexible. Start with small brush pens they give you more control when creating strokes.
Examples: Tombow Fudenosuke, Tombow Dual.

4. **Markers:** You can do calligraphy with a marker. Great for monoline, bold lines, and filling in large shapes. You can buy a set of Crayolas or a set of alcohol markers.

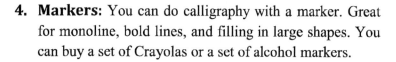

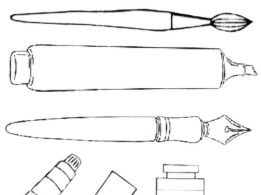

5. **Water brush:** The water brush pen is a great tool for any hand lettering and calligraphy work art. It allows to use different colors to paint or draw letters.

6. **Colored pencils:** Work good for many lettering styles when you start adding fancy decorative elements to your artwork.

7. **Ruler:** Use to create layouts & ensure measurement.

8. **Eraser:** For erasing pencil lineart.

9. **Paper:** Using the right paper can be as important as selecting your writing utensil. There are a variety of types of paper (printer paper, bleedproof paper, tracing paper, layout bond, ...) you can use different types of paper and different pens as long as you use the right pen for the right paper (Brush pen for smooth paper, Crayola markers on any paper).

REMEMBE

Make sure to invest in good quality materials, good quality doesn't necessarily mean expensive! You can find these materials at most art stores and online.

BODY POSTURE

When you're practicing calligraphy body posture is so important. Make sure you are comfortably seated and your shoulders are relaxed. Check your desk height and aim for your back to be straight. Adjust your posture every time and take breaks if you're tired. Get up and walk around, stretch your hand, rest your eyes for a while and return to your writing with renewed energy.

PEN ANGLE

How to hold the pen correctly?

The way you hold your pen is important when it comes to brush & hand lettering. Make sure you don't hold your pen at an angle that is too steep or too flat, but at a 45-degree between the pen and paper.

But different people like to hold the pen in different ways so this angle can vary with each individual, what's most important is that you find a grip that feels comfortable enough for you. A general rule is to hold the pen between the thumb and forefinger with some of the weight of the pen resting on your middle finger; and experiment with the angle a bit until you find the point where the ink flows freely and the pen travels smoothly across the paper.

Remember there is no right or wrong, these are just tips!

Practice makes perfect

BASIC STROKES

Congratulations on taking the first steps to getting started lettering! On the following pages you'll find practice strokes, practice as many times as you like to improve your muscle memory for key strokes. The basic strokes are the foundation of brush lettering. With these strokes, you can make every single letter. When practicing, remember to stay present, clear your mind and also feel accomplished by learning or improving on a new skill.

Recommended Tool: brush pen

BASIC STROKES

Follow and finish each basic stroke.
REMINDER: Upwards = less pressure / Downwards = more pressure

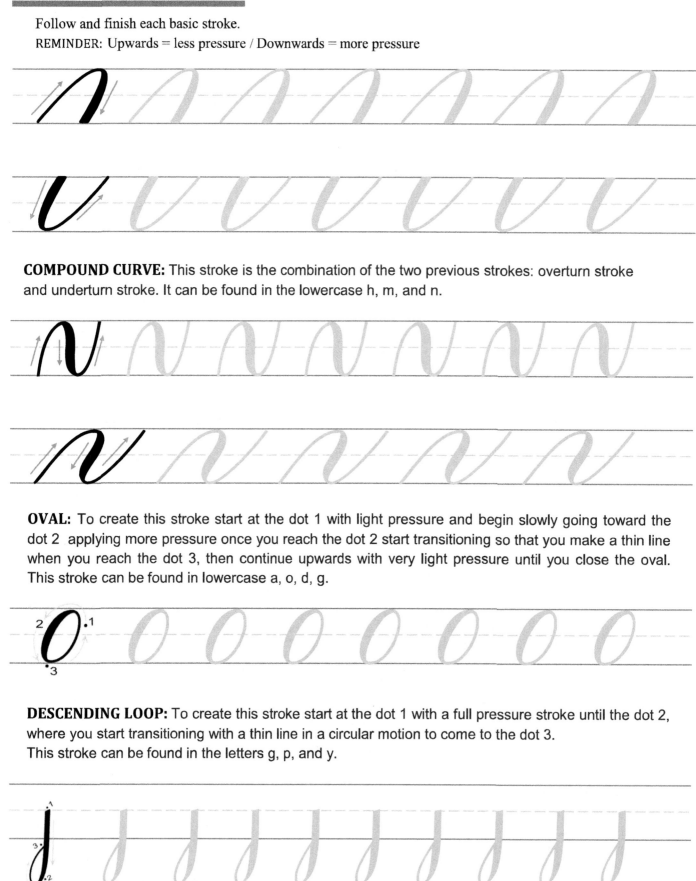

COMPOUND CURVE: This stroke is the combination of the two previous strokes: overturn stroke and underturn stroke. It can be found in the lowercase h, m, and n.

OVAL: To create this stroke start at the dot 1 with light pressure and begin slowly going toward the dot 2 applying more pressure once you reach the dot 2 start transitioning so that you make a thin line when you reach the dot 3, then continue upwards with very light pressure until you close the oval. This stroke can be found in lowercase a, o, d, g.

DESCENDING LOOP: To create this stroke start at the dot 1 with a full pressure stroke until the dot 2, where you start transitioning with a thin line in a circular motion to come to the dot 3. This stroke can be found in the letters g, p, and y.

MORE PRACTICE

The words "minimum" and "millennium" are great for practicing the upward and downward strokes.

Keep Practicing!

Set some time each day to practice! Grap a sheet of paper and keep tracing strokes until you feel confident

Now that you've gotten more comfortable with your strokes, we can begin forming letters. Think of each letter as a sequence of strokes. When brush lettering, unlike when we write in cursive (we tend to write fast and continuously), we write more slowly and we break each letter down into different parts, paying attention to each stroke. Most letters are built the same way: they are made up of the stem (vertical stroke) and a bowl (Like in a, b) or an arcade (like in m, n, w, u)

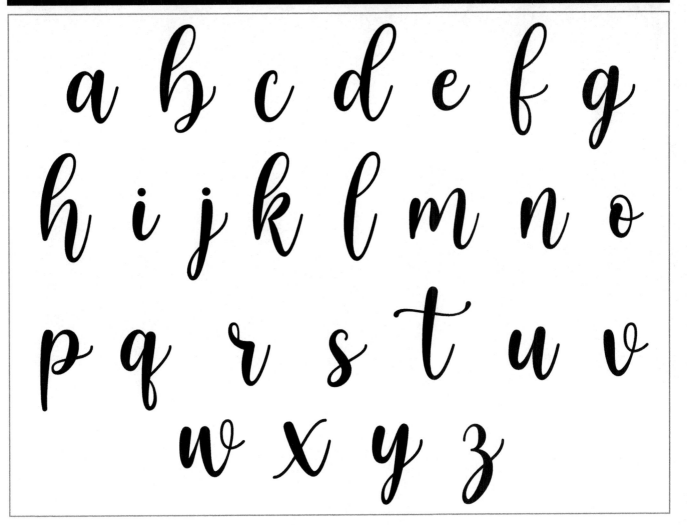

If we break the letter (a) down into strokes, it becomes an oval and a line downstroke.
Construct your letter by:
1) Create an oval to form the body.
2) Lift your pen off the paper at the end of the first stroke.
3) Finish your letter with a final downstroke.

Bowl: a stroke that creates an enclosed space (Like in letters a, b, d, g, and p).

● Starting point

BRUSH ALPHABET | LOWERCASE

a b c d e f g

h i j k l m n o

p q r s t u v

w x y z

BRUSH ALPHABET | LOWERCASE

Follow the arrows to trace the corresponding brush letters first, and then re-create your own on the blank space.
Recommended Tool: brush pen

BRUSH ALPHABET | LOWERCASE

i i i i

j j j j

k k k k

l l l l

m m m

n n n n

o o o o

p p p p

Remember!

There is no magic tool or paper that'll help you master the art of calligraphy, the secret is repetition. The practice will help establish muscle memory and help you get an idea of what each letter feels like.

BRUSH ALPHABET | LOWERCASE

q q q q

r r r r

s s s s

t t t t

u u u u

v v v v

w w w w

x x x x

BRUSH ALPHABET | LOWERCASE

y y y y

z z z z

A B C D E
F G H I J K
L M N O P Q
R S T U V W
X Y Z

Uppercase

BRUSH ALPHABET | UPPERCASE

Follow the arrows to trace the corresponding brush letters first, and then re-create your own on the blank space.
Recommended Tool: brush pen

J J J J

I I I I

K K K K

L L L L

m m m m

n n n n

O O O O

p p p p

BRUSH ALPHABET | UPPERCASE

Y Y Y

2 2 2

$$A \quad A \quad A \quad A$$

$$D \quad D \quad D \quad D$$

$$H \quad H \quad H \quad H$$

$$J \quad J \quad J \quad J$$

$$S \quad S \quad S \quad S$$

Monoline lettering is a fancy and elegant writing style in which the line remains the same weight from the beginning to end (There are no thick or thin parts in the letters).

This style can be created using any standard pen, pencil or marker; you do not need a fancy pen to make these letters (fine-point Micron Pen and Gelly Roll Pen both are beginner-friendly for monoline lettering).

It's great lettering style to play with when you find yourself stuck at the airport or in a waiting room.

MONOLINE ALPHABET | LOWERCASE

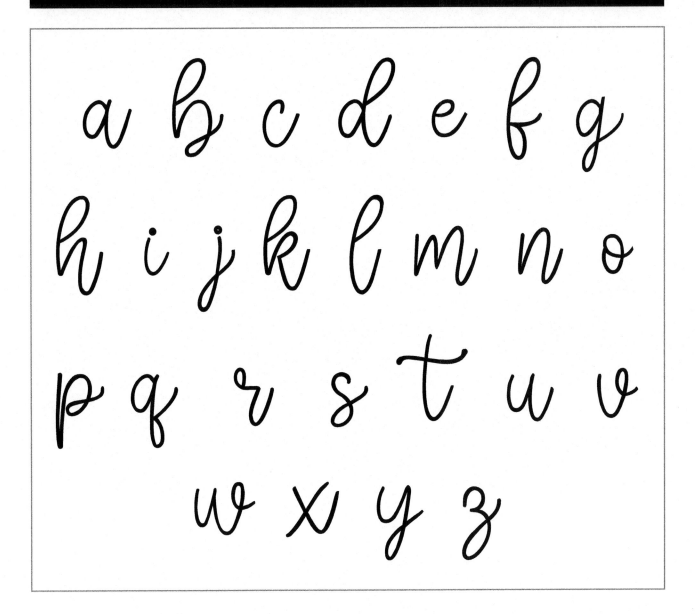

MONOLINE ALPHABET | LOWERCASE

Follow the arrows to trace the corresponding letters first, and then re-create your own on the blank space.
Recommended Tool: pen, pencil, or marker.

a a a a

b b b b

c c c c

d d d d

e e e e

f f f f

g g g g

h h h h

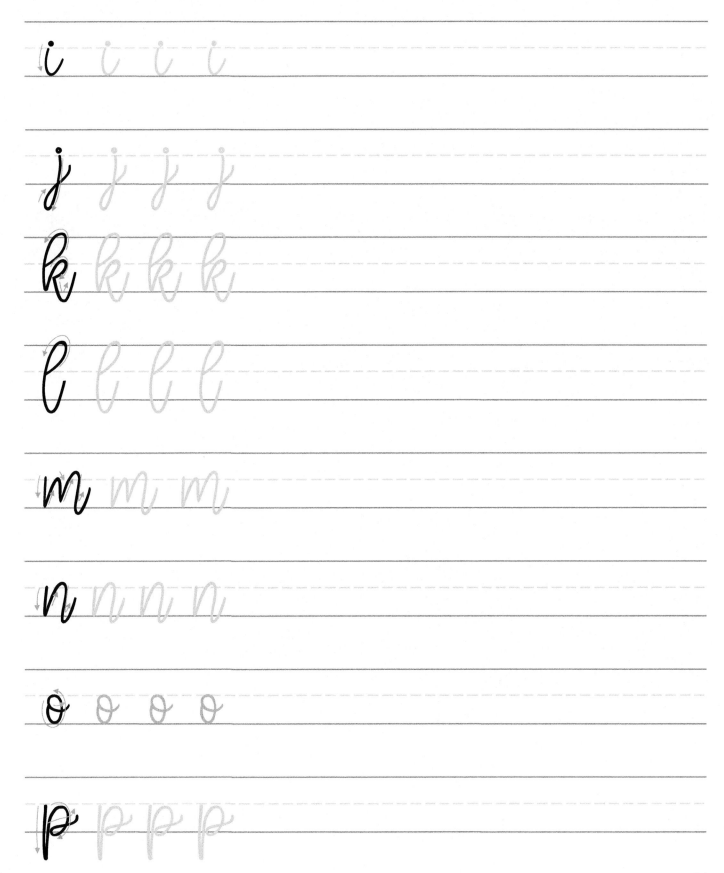

MONOLINE ALPHABET | LOWERCASE

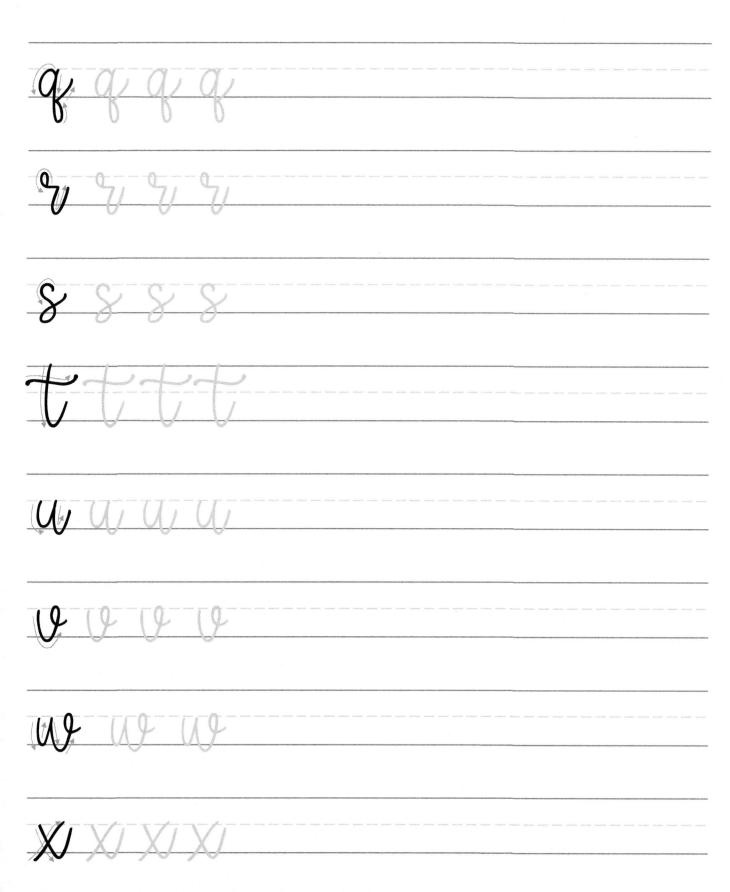

y y y y

z z z z

A B C D E
F G H I J K
L M N O P Q
R S T U V W
X Y Z

Uppercase

45

MONOLINE ALPHABET | UPPERCASE

Follow the arrows to trace the corresponding letters first, and then re-create your own on the blank space.
Recommended Tool: pen, pencil, or marker.

MONOLINE ALPHABET | UPPERCASE

Follow the arrows to trace the corresponding letters first, and then re-create your own on the blank space.
Recommended Tool: pen, pencil, or marker.

FAUX CALLIGRAPHY

Faux calligraphy offers a fantastic introduction to dip pen calligraphy. It will allow you to make beautiful lettering using any standard writing instrument like pens, pencils or markers before you attempt it with a dip pen. You may practice your faux calligraphy with any pen, on any paper you wish.

Also faux calligraphy gives you the ability to create lettering using a pen you're familiar with, so you'll be less intimidated to start learning. It will also give you the basics to learn letterforms and get comfortable with the thin and thick strokes.

This style is best for designs that call for an elegant or fun script, like wedding place cards or menus.

To create faux calligraphy, you'll first want to choose your writing utensil. It can be anything from a regular pen or pencil! Then:

1 **Draw your word in any lettering style you wish.**

You can write letters continuously, without picking up your pen during a word to keep things looking smooth, because moving too slowly can cause your lines to appear shaky.

2 **Find the downstrokes, and then draw lines to create the downstroke outlines.**

3 Fill in the downstrokes, and your faux calligraphy is finished!

TIPS TO CONSIDER:

1. Make sure you leave a fair amount of space between the letters! Otherwise the wider areas won't have enough space at the end.

2. It doesn't matter what side of the letter you draw in the parallel downstrokes on.

3. Any cursive writing can be transformed into faux calligraphy.

4. You don't have to fill in your faux calligraphy.

FAUX CALLIGRAPHY ALPHABET | LOWERCASE

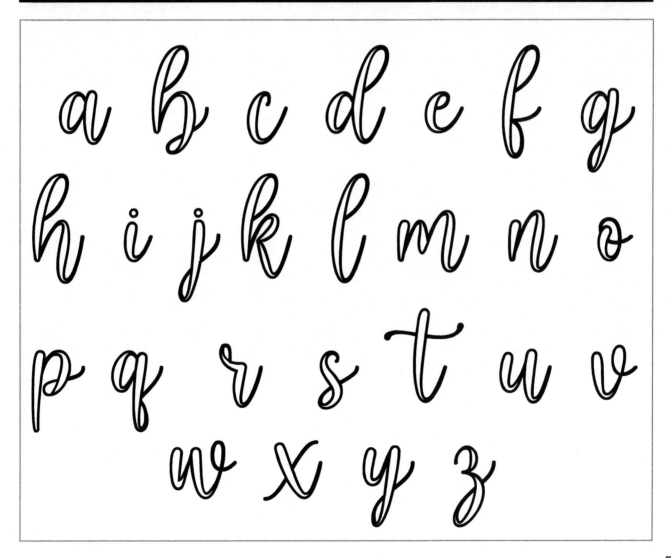

FAUX CALLIGRAPHY ALPHABET | LOWERCASE

Follow the arrows to trace the corresponding letters first, and then re-create your own on the blank space.
Recommended Tool: pen, pencil, or marker.

a a a a

b b b b

c c c c

d d d d

e e e e

f f f f

g g g g

h h h h

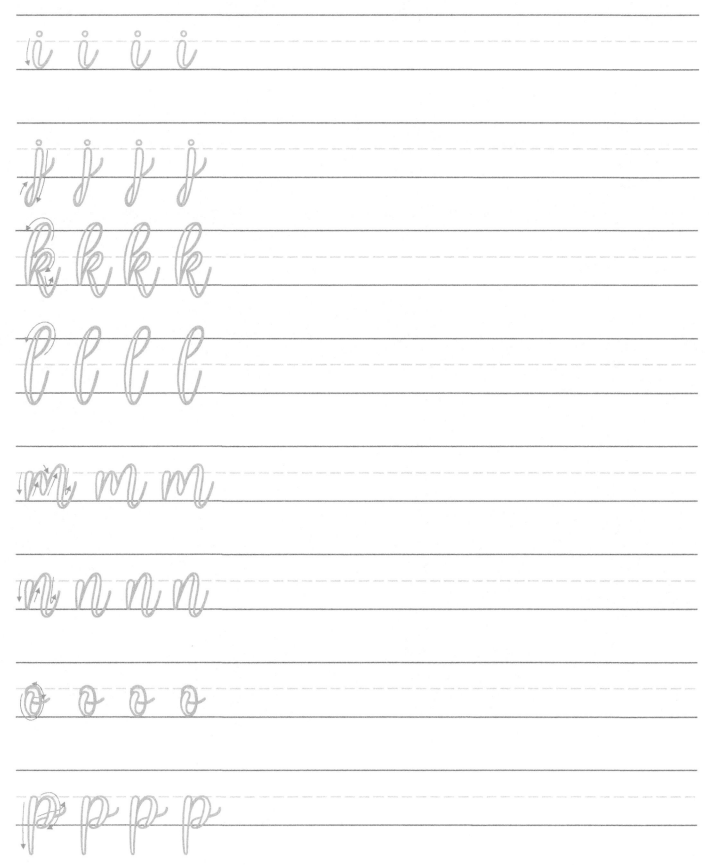

FAUX CALLIGRAPHY ALPHABET | LOWERCASE

y *y* *y* *y*

z *z* *z* *z*

FAUX CALLIGRAPHY ALPHABET | UPPERCASE

Follow the arrows to trace the corresponding letters first, and then re-create your own on the blank space.
Recommended Tool: pen, pencil, or marker.

y y y

2 2 2

FAUX CALLIGRAPHY

Is the best way to begin learning brush lettering because you can use any pen or pencil to create letters.

SANS-SERIF ALPHABET | UPPERCASE

This font style is widely used for emphasis (Headlines and road signs) due to its naturally black and bold type characteristic.

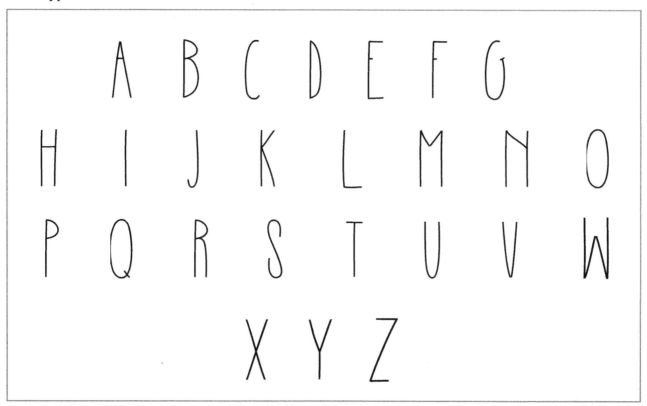

A B C D E F G
H I J K L M N O
P Q R S T U V W
X Y Z

SANS-SERIF ALPHABET | LOWERCASE

a b c d e f g
h i j k l m n o
p q r s t u v w
x y z

Serif is one of the oldest font styles and often used for body text because it's more legible and causes less fatigue to the viewer's eyes.

A B C D E F G

H I J K L M N O

P Q R S T U V W

X Y Z

SERIF ALPHABET | LOWERCASE

a b c d e f g

h i j k l m n o

p q r s t u v w

x y z

SANS-SERIF ALPHABET | LOWERCASE

Trace the corresponding letters first, and then re-create your own on the blank space.
Recommended Tool: pen, pencil, or marker.

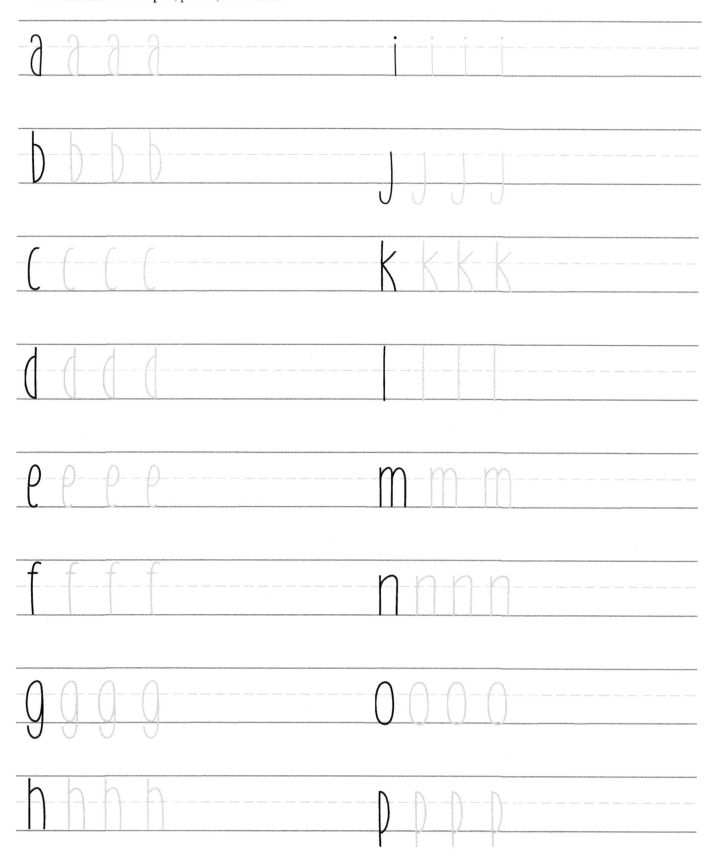

q q q q

r r r r

s s s s

t t t t

u u u u

v v v v

w w w

x x x x   y y y y   z z z z

SANS-SERIF ALPHABET | UPPERCASE

A A A A   I I I I

B B B B   J J J J

C C C C   K K K K

D D D D   L L L L

E E E E   M M M M

F F F F   N N N N

G G G G   O O O O

H H H H   P P P P

Q Q Q Q

R R R R

S S S S

T T T T

U U U U

V V V V

W W W W

X X X X   Y Y Y Y   Z Z Z Z

SERIF ALPHABET | LOWERCASE

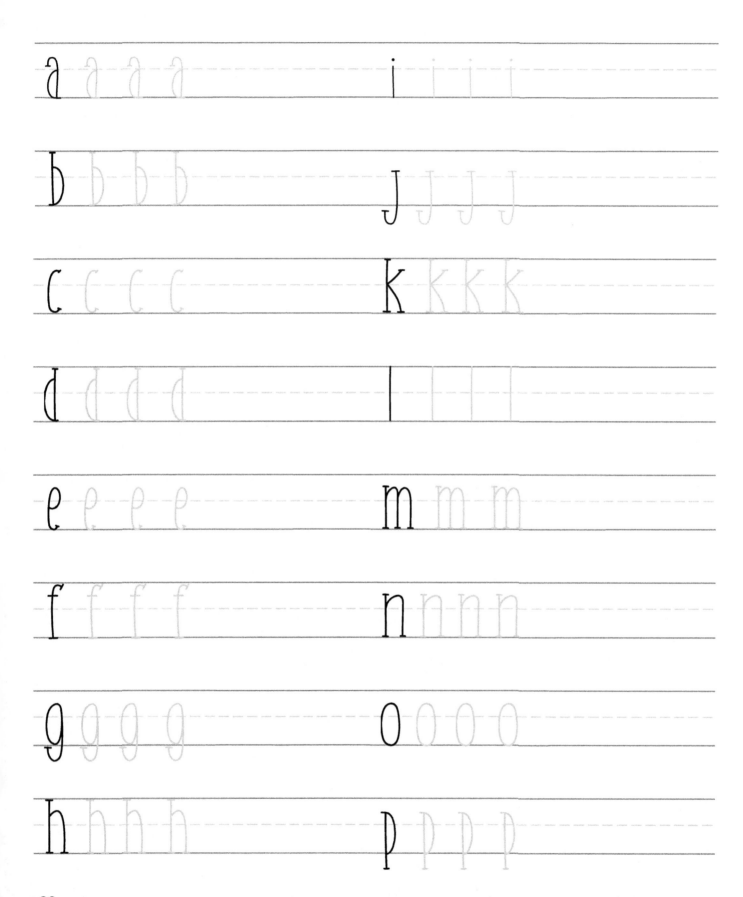

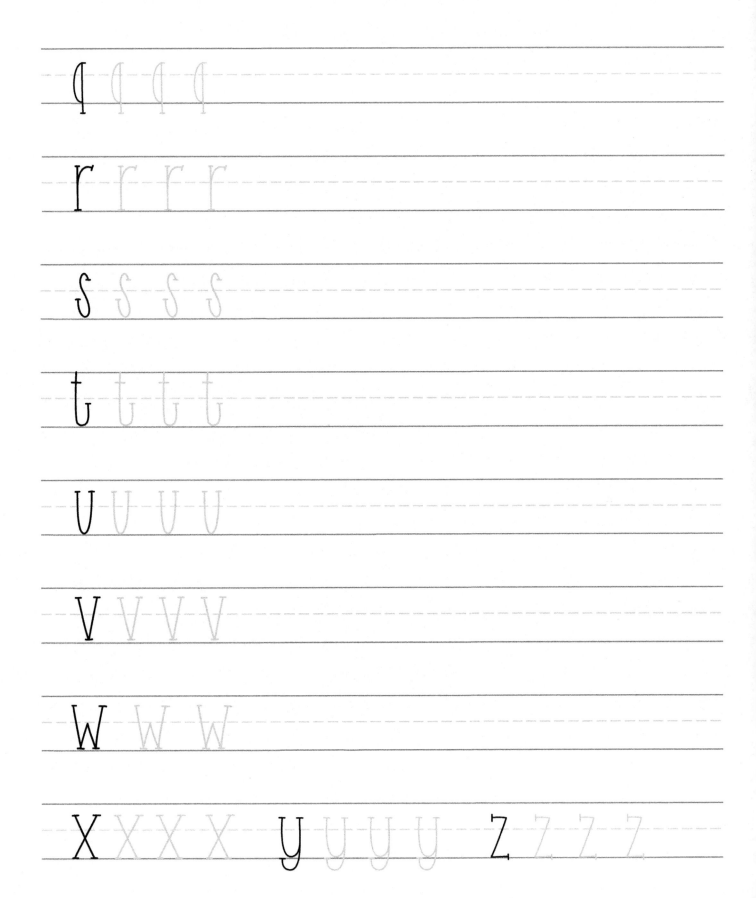

SERIF ALPHABET | UPPERCASE

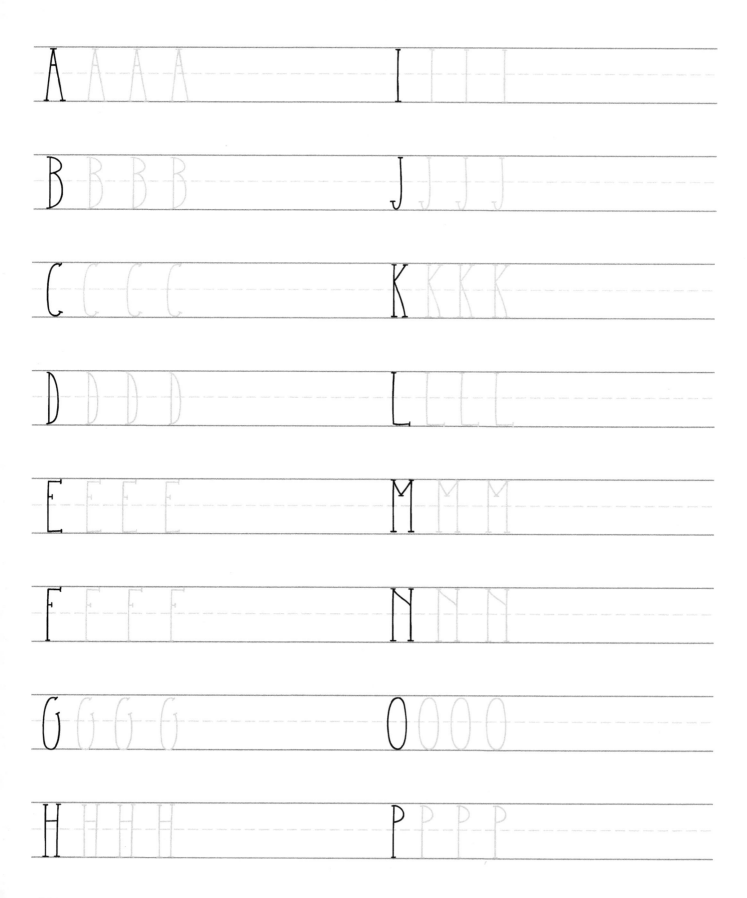

CONNECTIONS WORDS

CONNECTING LETTERS TO FORM WORDS

Now that you've gotten more comfortable with your strokes and letters, you'll now learn to connect letters to form words.

Here are some examples: "letter" , "writing"

Let's begin with the word *"letter"*

▶ Start your first letter " ℓ " . Take it up to your top line and then bring it down to the baseline. Finish your letter by lifting your brush up and to the right slightly to form a tail, and then take it up to the mean line (Form an exit stroke). This is usually where you lift your brush to form your next letter.

▶ Connect your next letter " e " to the tail of your previous letter by making sure your downstroke intersects the previous letter's tail.

▶ Continue forming your word by connecting each letter to the tail of the previous letter.

There are some tips to consider when you connect your letters:

● Think of each word as a sequence of strokes.

● Lift your pen off the paper at the exit stroke before beginning the next letter.

● Keep your connecting strokes consistent in length (keep the space consistent).

Do this *letter*   *letter* Don't do this

● Look at where you have cross strokes and use them to connect to other letters in the word.   *tt*

Lead-in and Exit Strokes: a slightly curved upstroke that begins at the baseline and goes toward the midline. Used to start and connect letters to make words.

LET'S CONNECT LETTERS!

Practice connecting letters, and then re-create your own on the blank space.

a b : ab

d e : de

c h : ch

l l : ll

d o : do

o n : on

m e : me

g h : gh

n l : nl

g n : on

t h : th

y p : yp

l f : lf

y o : yo

t l : tl

t t : tt

LET'S CONNECT LETTERS!

br : br

ve : ve

gu : gu

sr : sr

ks : ks

nl : nl

mi : mi

bx : bx

x r : xr

i x : ix

u y : uy

q p : qp

m z : mz

w n : wn

x y : xy

y z : yz

BRUSH LETTER WORDS

Now that you are comfortable with connecting two letters, let's learn to connect letters to form a whole word.
Use the arrows to trace each word first, and then re-create your own on the blank space.

kind *kind*

bride *bride*

love *love*

grace *grace*

make *make*

honor *honor*

glory *glory*

dream *dream*

BRUSH LETTER WORDS

hope *hope*

great *great*

beauty *beauty*

light *light*

think *think*

design *design*

happy *happy*

spirit *spirit*

BRUSH LETTER WORDS

admire   admire

bright   bright

enjoy   enjoy

courage   courage

progress   progress

freedom   freedom

gratitude   gratitude

wisdom   wisdom

BRUSH LETTER WORDS

improve *improve*

challenge *challenge*

beautiful *beautiful*

motivate *motivate*

adventure *adventure*

awesome *awesome*

congrats *congrats*

excellence *excellence*

MONOLINE LETTER WORDS

Now that you are comfortable with connecting two letters, let's learn to connect letters to form a whole word.
Trace each word first, and then re-create your own on the blank space.

look *look*

peace *peace*

high *high*

grow *grow*

style *style*

teach *teach*

smile *smile*

dance *dance*

MONOLINE LETTER WORDS

create create

truth truth

today today

inspire inspire

garden garden

darling darling

forgive forgive

control control

MONOLINE LETTER WORDS

hooray *hooray*

humble *humble*

mission *mission*

believe *believe*

passion *passion*

achieve *achieve*

vanilla *vanilla*

welcome *welcome*

MONOLINE LETTER WORDS

positive   positive

practice   practice

strength   strength

honesty   honesty

ambition   ambition

sunshine   sunshine

elegance   elegance

confidence   confidence

Embellishments
Illustrations

FLOURISHES & SWASHES

Now it's time to take your lettering to the next level! You can add flourishes anywhere in your hand-lettering work. Use a flourish to create an extra dimension to a word or quote, as the flourish creates a connective line from the letters to its embellished parts in a layout.

1 **Start by creating a draft of the word you will be using in any lettering style you wish.**

2 **Find spaces in the layout where flourishes can be added.**

3 **Experiment with different flourish styles and techniques.**

4 **Make sure your words are always readable. Avoid overly flourishing if it compromises readability.**

The word "flourishes" in its most basic form.

The word "flourishes" written with embellishments.

While there are endless possibilities with flourishing, it is important to understand that many variations are often extensions of simpler variations.

FLOURISHES & SWASHES

Trace the corresponding flourishes first, and then draw your own on the blank space.

FLOURISHES & SWASHES

hope

kind

love

bride

honor

glory

dream

happy

think

light

great

laugh

design

beautiful

FLOURISHES & SWASHES

look

create

truth

grow

welcome

FLOWERS & LEAVES

Adding flowers and leaves is an easy way to fill in large negative space around your words. Here are some samples of flowers and leaves that can be incorporated inside letterforms or as additional accents to your layouts.

LAURELS & WREATHS

BANNERS

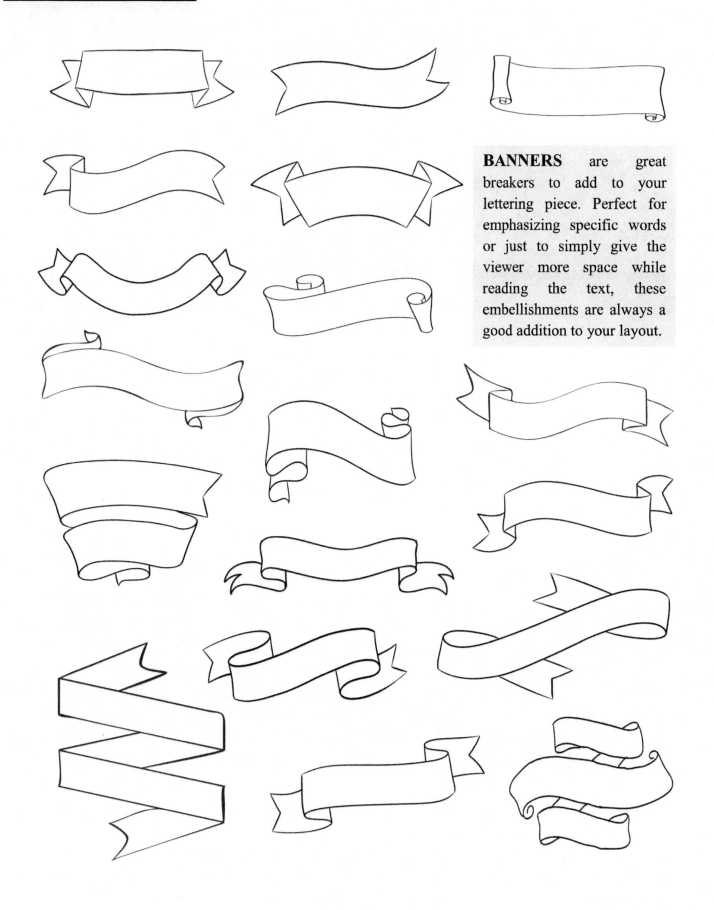

BANNERS are great breakers to add to your lettering piece. Perfect for emphasizing specific words or just to simply give the viewer more space while reading the text, these embellishments are always a good addition to your layout.

good

Design
Composition

COMBINING STYLES

You can always mix and match a bunch of lettering styles in just one design. But the simpler the style combination, the better and easier it is to execute. Stick to 2 or 3 font styles and keep your work neat and clean. As time passes and you keep practicing, you will learn what goes best with what, as well as develop your own style. Here are some lettering style combinations you can use:

Serif + sans serif

Serif + script

Sans serif + script

Serif + sans serif + script

YOUR DESIGN STEP-BY-STEP:

Great, you did it! You've made it to the final part of this book and have hopefully learned and enjoyed new knowledge about the art of hand lettering.

Here's where all of our elements collide creating your design. Everything from your kerning and baseline to your arrangement of words and decorative elements to create your final piece.

1 First, choose your piece, and then write it down with your normal handwriting. Underlining the words that you want to be emphasized. These emphasized words are the words that will carry the most weight in order to make your piece appealing and easy to read. Emphasizing the important words can be done in several ways by changing the size, style, or color.

"Make it happen"

2 Next, sketch out your design. Start by lettering the emphasized words first, and then fill in the rest of the supporting words. Experiment with different lettering styles that will go well together. If you are a beginner, you're better off keeping things simple and consistent (limit yourself to no more than 3 different styles).

Remember to use basic shapes to create your layout to eliminate unbalanced composition, and categorize words according to their strength and importance.

3 To put the final touches on the design, fill in the negative space around your words and add intricate details to letters. This helps to give the artwork more depth and enhancement. If you are satisfied with your layout design you can transfer it to a larger piece of paper for a good copy.

4 Once your piece is finished with pencil, revise until it looks the way you want. Then start to outline, add color, and finalize your design. The last step is to go back and erase your pencil lines once the ink has dried.

Now it's time to put it all to use in some projects! Use the next few pages to practice making some pieces. Start with tracing my design then continue to create projects of your very own with your newfound knowledge.

Be confident! Find your own path! Try new styles! Discover new things, mix up your styles, colors and writing tools to make beautiful final design.

PROJECT | 01

Trace the corresponding design "Be happy"

"Life is so beautiful"

"Make your progress"

"Merry Christmas"

PROJECT | 05

Trace the corresponding design "Best idea"

Now try to duplicate my design in your own step by step:

1. Write your quote in script (monoline)
2. Create the down stroke outlines
3. You can fill in the downstrokes, and your faux calligraphy is finished!

PROJECT | 06

"Don't lose yourself in your fear"

Now try to duplicate my design in your own.

"Good morning"

"You need to have fun"

"My best friends"

PROJECT | 10

"Light up the darkness"

PROJECT | 11

"Follow your dreams"

"Do small things with great love"

Printed in Great Britain
by Amazon

13782156R00072